APPEAL TO LANGUAGE

POEMS

BY

YANNIS PHILLIS

Translation by

Philip Ramp

Cyberwit.net
HIG 45 Kaushambi Kunj, Kalindipuram
Allahabad - 211011 (U.P.) India
http://www.cyberwit.net
Tel: +(91) 9415091004 +(91) (532) 2552257
E-mail: info@cyberwit.net

Printed at Repro India Limited.

For Sophia

Acknowledgement

Appeal to Language was first published in Greek by Enastron Publications, Athens 2019.

Poems of this collection have appeared in *Poetry Salzburg Review* and *Contemporary Poetry Vol. 3*.

Contents

RAIN IN ATHENS

Where are the rainy nights that cleanse the face
and return it to you in the morning eager
by a new adjective to be graced?

I followed the streets with a thin
film of the black mud that
forms after rain driven
by a thirst laying claim to my mouth.

Buildings were being vaporized by the night lights,
a din escaping from the city's depths.
On the corner of Patission Street
a beggar lay stretched out on the wet sidewalk—
one arm amputated at the elbow,
the other at the wrist.
His bare head scarred by an old burn
running down his face like an incoming tide.
He could have been an extraterrestrial
trembling from head to toe in his meager clothing
on those wet tiles.
His stumps set in bizarre positions
as if trying to protect himself from flames
or sending apocryphal signals
from his two-dimensional world.

I know how terribly cold the universe is
but I never cease marveling.

TIME

I never learned to calculate many things
not even the days the hyacinth always brings back
every January between two stones.
I am sitting at the small kitchen table
around which we then barely fit,
mother, father—five of us in all.
The mystery of space followed by that of time,
as one by one they left.
Now, alone, I'm in my old place cutting bread.
How many voices, how much laughter, how many
rituals does it take to nullify this void,
how many trials and errors were required
to settle me here on this speck of dust
in one of billions of galaxies.
Outside rain is dancing on a rosemary shrub.
I know it's not dancing for me nor for the blackbird
slinging tiny rainbows
from its lustrous plumage.

LERNA MILLS, 1825

June, the joyous month,
drawing from early on purple and blue hues upon the hills.
Wind swept through the narrow passage
brandishing dry cicada cries
and shrikes even drier ones
balancing themselves on thistles
oblivious to the multicolored crowd:
Egyptians, Turks, Philhellenes, Greeks
(it was hunting season then).

The first shots silenced the cicadas,
then the audacious birds
that were not aware of the strange roads desire takes.
Only the hollow booming of the cannons
reached the non-combatants in Nauplion
dragged there like ghosts
by the westerlies from the Mills.

The evening wiped away the booms, the cries, the dead.
The passage had a whole night lying ahead of it
before surrendering itself once more to insects and birds.

Years later, in the same place,
I did not reflect on any of that
my reason being
I had become absorbed by a robin redbreast
that itself was absorbed by an insect
and the sun was setting
behind a gossamer red cloud

and the meager light was learning to improvise
upon the farce of life.

They said a battlefield had once been there.

FROM CORINTH TO ATHENS

The national highway heads east.
Left a mountain chain made of dinosaur skin
right a sea of no originality.

Bus humming with kilometers.
The road binds me the world,
makes me part of it.
With the years I've learned
roads are not equipped with return,
that seasons arrive with a vocabulary all their own
and later are lost somewhere in the universe.

I am gazing at cypress trees through the window
as they hasten past like a film out of sync
bending to wind's whim.
For a moment I feel they are bowing to us as we pass
but know as well we are but a fleeting detail
in a landscape that converses solely with wind and rain.

COMMUNICATION

It's raining in Athens
and the city is donning its transparent mask
from the 20th century, a little out-of-date,
the worse for wear, but a mask nonetheless
ancient names themselves forgotten, dates
becoming street names before they faded away.
Anonymous citizens all
hastening to give their insignificant stories the slip
just as the superstitious do from ghosts.

The rain is transforming the city into a metaphor
as the drops tap out on the polished streets
their own code, one which no one will get
but the rain persists
for the sake of one lonely bitter orange tree on the sidewalk
which will shamelessly represent the world
the moment everyone has fled.

THE MAILMAN

And now as I recreate the world from memory
I hear the small brass bugle
summoning the village to its daily ritual of anticipation.
Two leather bags with letters from inside the country,
those from abroad colorfully striped,
the mailman always in the same khaki uniform,
his slender figure on a bicycle crowned by a chapeau,
a symmetry so hard to come by back then.

And now I am recreating the names from memory
as if the names he was calling
were from a list of souls—
brief lord of his small universe—
as he linked together two more points in the puzzle of communication
reducing it to lines and dots—
the perfect abstraction of his art.

When his mission was completed
he withdrew into his small house
to link the dots of his own life into lines,
the leather bag on his bike's rack bouncing about
joyously over all the places he's traveled to
by means of the senders' addresses,
the nights when the abyss lay heavy upon him
asking himself how a place grows smaller
with repetition
and then turns into a cocoon wrapped around him
something that for years he had seen set in relief in villagers' eyes
slowly reading the names
and now he could make it out clearly:
the absence of his own anticipation was not the work of memory.

MEMORY OF THINGS

I have seen the olive trees on the west coast of Crete,
bent by the relentless wind,
like the faithful prostrating themselves,
an elliptical landscape: ruffled bushes
rocks rusted, roar of the sea—
it's hard to speak in another language here.

These weird rocks, the crooked trunks,
bear the history of the wind and the sea
written thriftly but indelibly allowing for no other interpretations,
and escorting it through time.
I ask myself: until when?
I ask myself: is memory a metaphor?

I have no idea what I was looking for that afternoon.
My old friend
for years unable to communicate,
victim of a degenerative brain disease.
He looked at me for a fleeting moment and then his gaze
returned to his blank void.
His memory free to travel in space
I caught a glimpse of the galaxies it was crossing
the lack of anything written between.

BEE ON A PYRACANTH ON VOULIAGMENIS AVENUE

Endless traffic—spine of the avenue—
the vehicles, angry wasps
absorbed in their common purpose—
sun almost vertical, a light westerly.

The blurred image clears when we stop at a light
cleared as if by a lens focusing
on a single flowering pyracanth on that island
studded with white blossoms,
on ground otherwise strewn with cigarette butts, empty
beer cans and plastic bottles.
I observed the nervous bee cautiously examining
the blossoms, indifferent to the roar,
the westerly lightly ruffling its wings.

When we started moving again
I noticed the mangled guard-railing.
A driver had been killed.
In the weak night light
he wouldn't have seen the white blossoms
nor had time to imagine how that white
will turn into the harsh red of the pyracanth.

TIBET

Mountain peak and above it vultures drawing circles
before settling onto the naked dead bodies
the poor villagers had laid there for a sky burial.

Down by the river a mad hoopoe
flounders about in the breeze drunkenly,
rugged bushes dressed in purple flaunt the altitude.
I listen to the stories welling up from inside them.

At the large square Tsering
points out the places where monks immolated themselves.
At this altitude their cries can't reach our world,
lost in space and only returning later with the snow
to become part of the jagged glaciers.

An endless line of pilgrims along the sidewalk
hovering there in the incense smoke—
forming a line of anonymous apparitions
with only a worn bit of paper to serve as their ID.

At passport control
arrival without departure is not allowed.

I am in the country of nameless ghosts.

POTALA PALACE

A small grey bird is stumbling about through a straggly
clump of shrubs in a slight breeze,
framed by the dynastic walls
by which the palace is fringed.

The walls, riddled with windows,
summarize through colors what remains ineffable:
the difficult passage from the deep red of fire
to the white of knowledge,
after which the yellow of wisdom appears.
What color is the memory imprisoned in the sleepless building?

For a moment you think you are hearing God
as you are overcome by lightheadedness from a lack of oxygen,
the hard blue sky.

For that moment you think you are reading imperial dreams
in the reflections from the Lhasa river
the dreams of exile which are no longer dreams
and whatever was left of them:
ambiguous symbolic colors, incense smoke
yellow earth at the foundations,
the rubble of a bizarre craving.

ESCAPE

He left the southern seas behind him
the Great Barrier Reef—footstool of Queensland
before the coast yields to the Coral Sea.
From on high few details can be made out,
cities level with the ground, his wife, his five sons.
The mental hospital.
The airplane turns toward the Indian Ocean—
drone of the engines, a memory that's been suppressed.

The earth from this altitude looks smooth, almost azure.
At Harry Outpost in Korea in 1953
the earth shook off its skin and bared its black teeth,
clouds of steel, the defenders—
nocturnal roaches in trenches.
They said they were outnumbered thirty to one.
White flares were scorching the night
each morning the fallen bodies in their histrionic poses
the eyes of a fallen soldier filled with black dirt—
he closed them cursorily so they wouldn't be blinded by light so
harsh.

The plane is crossing parallels
till it reaches the sublime thirty-eighth.
The questions: first a volunteer in the *Sparta Regiment*
later an immigrant to Australia
to throw his shadows off the track.
In the psychiatric clinic there is a small sign with the notation:
Post-Traumatic Stress Syndrome,

the nurse who showed him how at night to take cover
from enemy fire pounding his Company.

Not even she ever learned how Antonis from Thessalonika
struggling to return to his childhood
one morning made his escape from human memory
on a scheduled flight
gone missing for thirty years now.

STORIES

These are your stories, they told me,
hurling me into the bizarre twentieth century.
I learned imitation and forgery—
it was easy I must confess.
Between the stories of war and incandescent iron
I squeezed in the hill with the ancient acropolis,
an enclosed sea, grey stones
that turn red in the afternoon
and the thyme riddled with holes by the wind.
There was also a rock—a figurehead flinging itself into the waves
and on it a lizard interpreting the sea warily.

They told me stories of eternity—
with time I forgot them.
The only thing remaining being I was too there
one more name, or better, event
without ulterior motive.
I no longer do forgeries
but looking back stick to training my memory
and imagination.
Science tells us one day everything will end.

SAN JUAN – PUERTO RICO

First came the tropical rain
polishing the stone lanes of the old city
sweeping from them History's heavy cloak.
Down on the shore, *El Morro* castle has surrendered to the sun
its enormous esplanade spread out before it
the sloping square that exposed attackers,
prey to the shelling from the castle.

In 1598 the English and in 1625 the Dutch
briefly inscribed on this square
the narrative of the Old and the New World:
fallen bodies in grotesque positions
unwieldy muskets, absurdly long swords scattered about.
What drives humans mad?

The din of the ocean came from the north
as we sipped our usual cocktail
from an unrestrained compulsion for power
and the harsh justice it gives birth to,
with a slice of precious metal on the rim of the glass.

Down on the shore at *El Morro*
couples were strolling
safely exposing themselves to the sun's fire
playing with their cell phone screens
texting brief messages.
They seemed to be tiptoeing
among the shadows of the English and the Dutch.

By sundown the crowd was hanging like marionettes
from the strings of the sun.
The sky had no further promises to death
or glory to keep
not even a storm to cleanse the memory.
A frigate bird had gracefully caught the wind
driving the waves
to the vulnerable side of History.

EASTER ISLAND

All night long the sea was roaring onto the shore
mercilessly pounding the black, abrasive lava
like a beast defending its territories from invaders
and Hanga Roa, the only village left on the island,
was voyaging with lights off in the middle of the Pacific.

In the past, ancestral spirits took the form of statues
to keep the dark spirits distant from humans.
Now without villages, without their coral eyes,
their huge empty sockets standing helpless
perhaps sad—all the statues equally blind.

In the morning the wind subsided
and the island once more donned its green overcoat
rent roughly by the ancient gaping volcanoes,
those tough and multicolored flowers of longing there.

For years you believed you had kept your demons at bay,
your vanity, your fears,
but in the end they returned without any resistance
to claim what belongs to them:
the empty gaze of anonymity that only love can repeal, and only
for a while.

When the sea started up again
the island was still resisting.
Light was slanting off the volcanic rocks—
ocean's eye wide open
clearing a way from the east
for the statues' final collapse.

SANTIAGO, CHILE

La Moneda means currency.
In Santiago,
in the La Moneda Presidential Palace
Allende was assassinated.
Before it became the seat of the President
it was a mint.

Neruda lived in Valparaiso.
There one night he wrote "the saddest lines."
Later poetry went postmodern
History the same
language, communication, the free market—
all became postmodern as well.

In Santiago the seasons are symmetrical
like pictures of inverted trees
on the shore of a lake.
To the East in the Andes the glaciers are melting
victims of climate change.
Down in Santiago a plane to Easter
Island, the Island of Statues
takes off,
slowly opening the Pacific as if it were a gate
and a white line like cast off skin follows it
during the time the stars turn from blue to red.
A crowd of tourists is taking pictures in front of the palace.
It's their only way of entering twice
that world where the palace has a symbolic name.

AUGUST, MIDDAY

The *meltemi* wind appeared suddenly out of nowhere
and without hesitation suffused the translucent shrubbery
at the edge of the shore
spreading a thin veil of dust over the white pebbles.
The wind pushed the sea southward
revealing passageways from green to dark blue
and the cane-brake that separated the lemon groves from the
melon fields
was bent over and whistling, resisting
and only two shrikes with their curt cries
struggled in that wilderness to impose their order upon the thistles.

People had departed. No one around to explain
this wind that was peeling the sea
and spreading with candor its dust over the works of humans
the passion of seasons that drove the migratory birds
from country to country.

While we were out in the middle of the sea—the only colonists in
the universe.
And I can still remember the acrid taste of salt on her body,
the concise language of our hands,
the brief eternity that midday set aside, just for us.

INK BOTTLES

I'm staring at pages left unwritten,
the ones that would bring me eternal or at least long-lasting fame,
I'm staring at the row of small ink bottles
like colorful troops on review,
the bottles of ink that never wrote the great epic
that would have made me immortal, whatever that may mean,
doing nothing more than making out the day's shopping list
the routine chores that had to be done by evening
some song lyrics that were heard between the waves of wind and
sea,
food recipes, a manual on repair of diesel engines.

I am staring at the small ink bottles
that every June have recorded the amount of oats and wheat
and in the fall the dates of the last harvest
and the winter plowing.

I spent some ink making mathematical symbols
that would explain a small part of the universe to me
but most of it I used writing notes
so I wouldn't forget the daily chores.
Here, for example, I recall my debt to a book seller
or the directions to a young woman's home
even the materials for the repair of my parents' home—
and they've been gone for several decades now.

I am once more staring at the pages that were left unwritten—
so much ink left unused.
I know that whatever I may do, immortality was a delusion,

a wonderful delusion I must confess.
As for the ink I'll be leaving it to my descendants
because I have no other use for it, nor want to.

DREAM

The dead always visit me at night.
At those latitudes the sun is merciless
which is why they always come at night.

I listen to them speaking with their new accent
I listen to their words
and only then invent everything they loved or hated
invent their questions, their steps taken,
their passions, their loves.
How else can I keep them on the side of memory
I need them to be?

During this season a wind came from every point on the horizon,
an implacable wind.

I watch them at night as they one by one pass by,
a procession of shadows
and know the time has come.
The words, the accent, the faint sound left by their steps on the
ground
the crackle of leaves under their soles
the passions, the loves—
the time has come to board the well-known boat
one enters once and once only,
the ancient river of Lethe.

WALLS

Tonight I'm reflecting on the fact I've spent nearly my whole life
between walls, perhaps because it couldn't have been otherwise
just as a word cannot be written outside the alphabet.

There were many walls:
those people pray before
and those that divide people into races,
walls we call home.
There were also those with works of art, walls colored,
white, empty,
walls of camps or of prisons
walls of educational institutions.

There are genera and species of walls.
Walls evolve just as species do,
come into being and becoming extinct as species do, too.

Tonight I'm reflecting on the wall opposite me
with photos of people on it—
most of them departed for years now.
Only their ephemeral smiles have remained
fossilized, almost real.
I gaze at their military uniforms, their suits,
old-fashioned dresses,
struggling to make out the terror
of war behind those smiles,
that ravenous desire
for a momentary escape from the continuity of time
the hail! bestowed on them by a camera's flash.

Tonight I am reflecting on the wall that down through the years
and without marble slabs, crosses and classical inscriptions
has become a cemetery for all the names I still do remember.

A WORLD WITHIN THE WORLD

Jasmine. Amid its white flowers
a grey finch pays tribute to its refracted light
with all the syllables it knows between s and r,
casting fleeting glances
at the outside world still struggling
between paradise and hell.

SILENCE

We were sitting on the trunk of a fallen tree
as the slanting light of November
X-rayed the stripped pomegranate trees at the fence
a year before he departed with the same simplicity
that afternoon offered up its place to the twilight.

I asked him about Asia Minor in 22
Rimini in 44
His answers brief as the final line of a poem.
He had no other way.

Years later and fallen trunk in exactly the same place
bearing witness to a landscape that changed as slowly.
By then I'd learned that only through silence
are the hardest stories told.
Leaving the mystery of time:
the questions that have found no answers,
the shadow that grows longer year by year
there amid the grass the trunk is now covered with
the sudden departure of my father
which too gave its place to that silence unlike any other.

THE TORTURER OF 1967

Four decades later
I saw the bent old man
with a plastic bag of medicine in his hand.
There was once the figure whose unwrinkled
major's uniform then fit him to a T
with its colorful medals, its phoenix on military hat
worn pulled down hard, the motionless predator's stare
underneath the visor as in a thunderous voice
he spread fear through the torture chambers.

The old commander wanted to become a hero. Ended up a
shadow.
His works had no originality he merely repeats.
Perhaps might fill a page.

To whom should be rendered what was owed?
How can such a debt be repaid to those who have since de-
parted?
To the people whose faces lie in ruins
and the orphan cries wandering here and there every anniver-
sary?
He can't even remember the moment when glory became a
tumultuous fall.

Memory is always a selective thing.
He never said how he would endure the final anonymity
nor if he knew the distance between
the lie and justice
the distance between the wrong choice of words
by which humans are separated.

THE OLD CANNING FACTORY

I experienced my first images of the century
through the voices of the female workers
arranged along the benches of the canning factory,
the noise made by the machines
each one with its own unique signature sound.

I experienced the erotic atmosphere in the steam,
furtive glances, the girls' faces done up with the sun's makeup
two buttons left open on blouses as if forgotten about.

The shrill whistle of the immense steam boiler at night opened a
way
for itself between the cries of the owl
and the sea further down surrendered itself to the slabs
only to later wake up like a beast from its winter hibernation.

I read the syntax of the past:
the way the phrases were oxidized
to which they lent the form they desired.

I experienced an obsolete century.
I experienced what I experienced without going back
and then one July afternoon
I turned back for the last time
and ran by hand over the old machines one by one
the monstrous press, the vertical can sealer
the pumps and the pipes—
arteries which once carried life—

the benches left behind the scenery forgotten from bygone
performances.

How quickly the smooth surfaces
took on a grey patina of dust
and the belts became eaten away like dead spider legs
without purpose there in the meager light
coming through the warped windows
scattered about with the rough clarity
of fleeting haloes.

STORIES OF GREECE

The investigation of names is the beginning of education.

Antisthenes

The first duty of the true leader is the restoration of names

Confucius

A. Prologue

Because words carry weight
because lies are told with words
because liberty is disfigured by words
because words give birth to injustice
I said I would follow the way of narration
without the burden of outmoded embellishments
without hackneyed evasions
without bloated incomprehensible forms
without half-truths.

So I said I would start with language
because the truth is only revealed in the presence of language
and things are better understood if left unsaid
and poetry is the art of leaving things ineffable.

Better one precise word than a blinding flare.

Because the era of superior races has returned
corrupted narratives have also returned
the debased books containing the skeletons of History.
Because the shameless language of public discourse has returned
because the investigation of names
has never been sufficient to give language a just rendering
a justice like the one a bee today conferred on lemon blossoms
and hastily restored by intuition the names it knew.

B. The early years

My first words were taught me by the Heracleian stones of the
ancient acropolis
and the flat tiles with their mossy surfaces
and the hidden coves with their little fish and shrimp,
back then when the world was made of two arteries of water
connecting land and sea
three transitory lagoons and two barren islets
set in the mouth of a bay leading to infinity
and a woman's white, pure white, body
that I still didn't know how to read.

Thunderbolts came early to recreate
the world from its primal matter
and then deconstruct it showing no mercy
as I began struggling even then
to find its place in the order of names.

And the beginning of things, a pan-earth of intuition
a pan-sea made of those same first words,
so wanting, so beautiful!
And how strange when explanations grew fewer
and things made their escape between questions
that increased rather than diminished
because when the world inundates you
you have no idea where logic and that something other are
that which is not spoken of with numbers or other human means.

How do you enter a miracle without exiting from it?

The light is not always gentle
because light does not reveal the truth but stresses the shadows.
And there at the Heracleain stones I read the first scripts
and saw the works of humans from thousands of years before
and nothing was left but a few bushes, some ruins,
there where the sea sets its limits shamelessly
and the mild south wind is spreading its mist.

C. The first stories

A map placed on a school wall
Dervenakia, Alamana, Maniaki
and the north wind whistling unimpeded through the warped
windows
making us more vulnerable to these stories of glory
under the merciless gaze of an icon hanging on the wall.

He swayed a little like the laurel bushes in the yard
and then collapsed on the floor
as the teacher gave him a violent shove
and set his foot upon him like a triumphant hunter
because the young pupil had not known the answer to a question.
His spasms raised small clouds of dust
and made lovely designs in the slanting light.

Then came the lineage and species of names
used to classify things
and find their place in human ideas.
It was then I learned the world is divided and united by names
that people tear down and build with stories.

So I took the well-known roads
between chance and necessity
my tool made of whatever was left from benevolent peace of
oblivion:
stories of wind and stone.

And I am now writing this amid the sounds of night
which are not the sounds of triumphant drums

nor the din of a great battle
nor the vibrating voice of an important demagogue or dictator
but rather night sounds and it does not change
as the fact I am now writing does not change
drawing out of the dust books of time
scattered insignificant words
without which the world cannot be made.

D. A convenient world

People had become accustomed to the tyranny of large numbers
following the two wars—
the dead, the missing, the uprooted.
Now they needed even larger numbers
to reinvent hope.

In the school a warped desk, paint badly faded
the blackboard limitless.
They taught us that the earth lies at the center of the universe
and we are its chosen inhabitants
destined for eternity—
a large number simply inconceivable
if the story were to have a happy end.
I still remember the wild joy that filled me
listening to stories of supreme powers
who violated the laws of nature.

A few years later I alighted from the clouds
and read the world's writing from the start.

I like the small numbers
those that reveal the unbearable truth
with the limited steps I am able to make
and today I saw an insect reading the flowers on a cactus—
how can one correct such a picture?
The flowers retain the memory of the sun
thus giving me a little time to copy them.
Only thus do I have any hope of writing a clearer narrative.

E. Ethnogenesis

The seas in these parts remember winds
as they beat upon the turf of humanity, gives it shape
and then abandons it to the mercy of the elements.

When tribes came south
they brought with them the hunter's cry
and terrifying gods who had made the world
of fire and stone.

Then, by means of stories and names, they invented
places for everything.
They carved on stone and wrote on papyrus
The Odyssey, Antigone, The Elements
and that great *On the Sphere and Cylinder.*

And Thucydides, well-aware of History's selective memory,
preserved it in his *Dialogue Between Athenians and Melians*
and later Alexander the Great leveled Thebes to the ground.

Thousands of years have passed
while the paradox at civilization's foundations remains the same,
the ratio between sword and reason unchanged.

And I have seen people
who still converse with statues.

F. Byzantium

Byzantium, its walls running from the airport to Taxim square,
signs in Turkish, demonstrations
and centuries ago, fantasies of an empire: the language, Greek,
religion, intrigues, glories, conquerors, assassins, slaves
and before that a colony: seamen with a skin of salt, merchants
and before that a piece of land for larks, for crows,
for north winds.

There is no weather report for History
as we never learned to distinguish dust from stone.

G. Turkish Occupation

The Polis has fallen.
And the only thing I can imagine is the geometric shapes faces
took.
I am speaking of the vanquished—
the fierce faces of the conquerors do not concern me.
How many days and nights can a face endure before it falls
apart?
Does terror have a shape?

During those years the distance between the living and dead
was at most the length of a stone wall of a castle,
at most a smattering of simple phrases like those we hear today.
For example: *God is great!*

History is written gradually.
Between its lines a lining of
convenient lies and equally convenient truths
hard to tell apart from typos
or sentences subjected to censorship.

A human herd—a slow procession
moving through the dark for around four hundred years.
I said I can imagine that. Nothing more.

One hundred and ninety six years after Greece was liberated
from the Turks
I am watching the parade on the 25th of March.
A jaunty band is strutting proudly down Panepistimiou St.
At Zonar's cafe its patrons are absorbed in their discussions.

A homeless man wrapped in his rags is sleeping on the sidewalk—
in the filthy bundle only his head can be seen.
I don't need to imagine one thing more nor add a single word.

H. German Occupation

1941, strange. 1942, equally strange.
There was no ink for one to record the images:
the dead man with a grimacing smile
leaning against the lovely marble of a neoclassical building
as if resting,
the frozen bodies on a truck bed.
There was no ink to describe the pain of hunger
the extravagance of ten soldiers to execute one citizen,
the trains heading north,
the fleeting eyes behind the bars of the cars.

Statistics is the art of averages
and History the art of statistics:
casualties in hundreds of thousands,
tons of gold, daily train schedules.

Cold nights, deserted streets
but the frozen bodies always managed to find a place on the
sidewalks for themselves
leaving spaces for the carts, the rickety trucks come morning.

Nights in Athens were white that winter.
White contains all the colors
the same way the faces of those soon to die
contain all the questions
for which there was no ink for anyone to record.

I. Civil War I

From the hilltop across the way could be heard isolated
machine gun bursts almost unreal
as three partisan women chatted under an old oak
about a few minor wishes of theirs.
The one wanted a slice of a herb-pie,
another a plate of roast lamb and potatoes
Maria wanted a door knob, a door. A home to come to.

When the mortars of the National Army began shelling
her wounded husband crawled into a cave,
Maria kneeling at his side with a new born child.
She surrendered with her child.
She never learned when the coup de grâce was delivered to her
husband.
If he heard her cries
if they left him face down on the ground
or on his back, eyes wide open
staring at the blackened ceiling.

It was the period directly after the great flood
and Deucalion strode upon the hard earth
and people became stones
men women children returned to the earth
and became stones.

J. Civil War II

He moved quickly among the gorse and grey stones
toward a clearing with olive trees on the mountain top
as if he were dancing the *Syrtos* on Easter Sunday in the village
square.
He was taken from his home at night, *for a brief interrogation,*
by two gunmen from the *Organization for the Protection of the
People's Struggle*
with the absolute authority invested in them by their ideological
orthodoxy
as to who they called *reactionaries.*

What might the second lieutenant of the Albanian Front have been
thinking
in the clearing with the olive trees
with his expressionless judges fallen silent?
Perhaps the assault of his platoon at the front
on the snow-covered battlefield against the Italian shelling
or the meager crop of wheat from his stony field
because that winter there had been no rain
or perhaps a woman's body—a painful fantasy?

They found him face down in the morning in his blood.
Two stray dogs were pulling at his tattered pants.
At the church they dressed him in his officer's uniform
buttoning it all the way up to his neck
to hide the black slash on his throat
so deep it drowned his last attempt to try and understand.

K. Dictatorship

If I had not felt the steely look of the torturer
as he checked people at the gate to the Polytechnic School
if I had not seen people turned into shadows
in the cells where Athens was proudly writing its new history,
I would say what happened in April 1967 was a comedy
one more ridiculous military maneuver
played out on the field of some glorious fantasy:
the performances, the slogans,
the misprints of the 20th century, so boring, so trite,
the uniforms, the vestments, those missing—
only the mad don't give a damn about the coming day.

Eight years later a court demoted the colonels
to privates.
Later on, one by one they disappeared into oblivion.
Without their military ranks once down in hell
how were they to order their lieutenants
to drive their armor
into one more parody of an advance,
how were they to order their sergeants to dispense their justice
made from an old fashioned form of terror?

I don't know what remained from all that.
The torture chambers were renovated turned into offices.
Only at night do some still see
the dark silhouette of a sentry at the gate,
hear his heavy boots on the cement.
The asphalt bears no scars of armored tracks
in winter there are fewer starlings in the trees.

All those who still remember say little
so they are able to return to the beginning of things.
Memory without imagination is missing something.

L. Economic Crisis

People have many needs
the need for a loaf of bread
the need for a luxury car
the need for investors to invest in the markets
the need for posthumous fame
the need of a homeless person on Stadiou St. for a dirty blanket.

The system working automatically in accordance with the rules of
the market:
at daybreak billions start being transferred across screens
and entered on computer hard drives
in the form of binary digits.
At the same moment the supply and demand of goods are being
balanced.
Food and housing are among these goods
that are also reduced to binary digits.
Come evening the numbers are added up algebraically
with a positive or negative sign.

Every morning a story is recorded in memory
like rings on the trunks of trees.
The insects that will inherit the earth are waiting patiently.

And on this cold night a homeless person
turns to the wall in the illusion of being at home
and to keep the bright city lights
from smacking him in the face.

M. Climate Change

Years later the dust blanketed the city,
blanketed the trees and the houses,
the dust of the Sahara driven by visible winds,
dust, that most patient of teachers
covered people, emptied their faces
later covering their chronicles with an opaque veil.

It was a story better told by numbers—
emissions of greenhouse gasses, rise in temperature—
numbers demand their own special imagination
if they're to give a shape to the future.
For this was a story with thousands of others enclosed within it.

The world, it is said, is made of love,
the world, it is said, cannot end.
And the way it is said you'd think the outcome of a soccer game
was being predicted.

Let us then go to the new world,
to the hours that bear the weight of centuries,
to the faces with the weight of salt.

On all souls day no one will cry for us.

Because I have seen exotic cities become lost in monsoons
as if they were old sailing ships in the open sea,
and have also seen mountains shedding their glaciers
as if they were baring themselves before an unknown conqueror
out of fear,

I have seen islands slowly kowtowing to the horizon's waterline.
Because I have seen the numbers and this is the simple truth.
And there is nothing metaphysical in the collapse of a civilization
or rhetorical in the question: shall we continue the intoxicating
dance or abandon it?

N. Appeal to Language

I would like to learn one or two things by means of their names.
For example, the word ink
which doesn't mean water or sea or even rain.
It only means ink.
With ink you write.
The word ink has no antonym.

I don't care about the word television.
Television is a three-dimensional multisided object
which sometimes fabricates news and other times commercials.
Nor am I interested in the word politics.
Politics is a modern profession
that nullifies what the polis postulates.

I want to learn one or two things unequivocally
such as a pomegranate bursting in fall
a blue wooden door,
or a door knob or even a shopping bag
maybe even a scooter with ball bearings
one of those kids learn how to balance on.

I also want to learn one or two things from their opposites.
For example, the word threat
or the word vague or the word lie
and in the same way mariners learn reefs by heart
and hurricanes by name.

I want to say that the wrong language is the lack of language.
I want to say that language is not a euphemism.

O. Epilogue

So then. As the lights are lowering pensively
I have told the tale of my brief appeal.
Now I'm wondering how this narration will end.

I have always kept count of solstices—
the way justice is conferred upon light
by the small planet I happened to be on.

I have slept under the stars and the silhouette of a scops owl
I have seen sea shores change by the hour
rivers dividing up the earth and then disappearing
and I have seen the shadows of people lengthen
in line with the determinism that rules the ages.
I have heard the truth told by next to nothing.

I have read maps with borders, mountains ranges with owners
seas divided by broken lines.
The maps contain no symbols for the rotting climate
for nature deadly still. Maps speak only half truths.
The other half left to language
to find the way on its own.

I know I need to find a way out and quickly
a couple of excuses to carry on
that is why I call on the robin redbreast and the European roller
a field rife with poppies
what is not yet ripe but so full of anticipation
body of a girl on an ancient shore.

The sun appears from the east revealing the sea before it
the sea then reciprocates.
On the rocks salt, footprints of the Sirens.